MURDER TONIGHT!
Rehearsed Improvisation on a Theme

by
Ian Wilkes

**IAN HENRY PUBLICATIONS Ltd.
PLAYERS PRESS**

MURDER TONIGHT!
Rehearsed Improvisations on a Theme

ISBN 0 86025 460 7 U.K.
ISBN 0 88734 904 8 U.S.A.
Library of Congress Catalog Number: 94-12441

IAN HENRY PUBLICATIONS, Ltd.
20 Park Drive
Romford, Essex RM1 4LH
UNITED KINGDOM

and

PLAYERS PRESS, Inc.
P. O. Box 1132
Studio City CA 91614-0132, U.S.A..

© Copyright, 1995, by Ian Wilkes,
and PLAYERS PRESS, Inc.

ALL RIGHTS RESERVED; no part of this
publcation may be reproduced, stored in a
retrieval system, or transmitted in any form
or by any means, electronic, mechanical,
photocopy, recording, or otherwise, without
the prior permission of the Publishers

Simultaneously Published
U.S.A., U.K., Canada and Australia

Printed in the U.S.A.

Library of Congress Cataloging-in-Publication Data

Wilkes, Ian.
    Murder tonight!: rehearsed improvisations on a these / Ian Wilkes
  p. cm.
ISBN 0-88734-904-8
1. Dinner theater - United States.   2. Improvisation (Acting)
3. Detective and mystery plays - Stories, plots, etc.   I. Title.
PN2270.D56W55   1994
792'.022--dc20   CIP
                                                                    94-12441

INTRODUCTION

Most drama groups have used improvisation as a tool for extending their knowledge of the dramatic art, but the sad thing with improvisations is that they are generally for `internal use' only and, however good they are, are rarely seen by people outside the group.

Here is a series of improvisations that are aimed specifically at public showing and participation. Of course, they will need to be rehearsed and so might not properly be called improvisations at all - although what happens during any one performance is in the lap of the Gods.

The basic requirement is a dinner situation; this might be in a restaurant or hotel on an `ordinary' evening, at a private party or at a parish wine and cheese. The main essential is that the drama group/participants are not known to the other guests, otherwise the sustaining of a character becomes well-nigh impossible. Alternatively, the group might like to play the game amongst themselves and assemble the ten for their own dinner party at the home of one of them. In this case, of course, the participants should be even deeper into their characters and keep them up through thick and thin for the whole evening.

The setting up of the venue for the evening is probably the single most difficult aspect of the enterprise. The `selling point' is that a thrilling and, hopefully, amusing entertainment will be presented to the other diners, who might be encouraged to pay a premium for attending a Murder Dinner or, at worst, it might be staged on an evening that the restaurant regards as `slow' - if a restaurant owner can fill his establishment on a Tuesday when otherwise he might be lucky to have four covers, he might well be interested in hosting and advertising the `show'. What the drama group could hope to get out of it - apart from the experience - could be, at least, a free meal, maybe with a small fee for funds as a bonus.

The basic skeleton of the Murder Dinner is that a group of people assemble for a meal and, at some stage during the proceedings, one of them has to be carried out prone! Foul play is suspected and either a policeman (who is another member of the drama group, who has had to hang around out of sight) is brought in to solve the mystery or one of the group assumes control and conducts the investigation. The paying public is invited to help the interrogator by inquisitioning the group members (except, of course, for the victim) one by one and table by table and then the interrogator asks a further set of questions, aimed at further revealing the backgrounds of the group members. Then, armed with substantially more information, the public is invited to ask individual members a few more questions and, finally, they are asked to decide who did it and why. Everyone except the criminal must have answered all questions truthfully within character. The person who selects the murderer and who gets nearest to the motive is declared the winner and is awarded a suitable prize.

It is essential that all the drama group know exactly who they are, what relationship they hold with other group members within the improvisation and that they can establish a *rapport* with the guests, both to tell their own story to them and to, maybe, cast suspicion on other cast members!

The only cast member who cannot be either the murderer or the victim is the investigator: apart from him or her it is suggested that the producer tell the individuals who are to be the two principle participants of their particular rôle in private shortly before the `performance', so that no other member of the group (and possibly not even the investigator) will know who the murderer is - nor yet the victim, until he/she takes a dive into the blancmange, gets carried out and then is announced by a grave restaurant manager as having died in his arms. If the group is performing an `internal' murder just among themselves, again the producer (who should not be present at either sort of event) will have put the `black spot' on investigator, murderer and victim unknown to the remainder of the group.

The following structured improvisations offer a setting, characterisations for each of the participants and a selection of questions that the investigator might ask to bring out the various relationships. The first example is worked out in some detail - after that only the bare bones are suggested for the group to flesh out themselves. In most cases the group is of ten people, but groups can add or deduct members according to their own membership - remembering to also add a suitable `biography' or spreading the relevant biographical details of the deleted individual around the remainder, if necessary. Almost invariably, the method of despatch would be poison - other methods tend to be difficult to pull off realistically when in close proximity to an audience.

The average cast make-up in the following scenarios is ten, 4/5 men 6/5 women, but a number of characters in most improvisations could be of either sex and still remain credible; although some adjustments of the biographies might be necessary.

Positioning of the group will have to be carefully thought out. It doesn't matter if they are in the middle of the room, or at the side, but they should not be placed deliberately away from the other diners and certainly not in any sort of stage setting on a dias or isolated at the further end of the room.

Obviously, they must be in character from their first entrance - which will possibly not be as a whole group, but they might `dribble in' to their table as do most of the other parties. Once in position they should not go out of the way to draw attention to themselves, unless one or more of them sees this as essential within his/her improvisation. Maybe they will be talking (in character, of course) a mite louder than any other table in the room, but they should not be the centre of attention - until the unhappy event which propels them into the limelight.

The only other question is at what part of the evening that unhappy event does take place. This is, of course, up to each invidual producer, but the most auspicious time is probably during the dessert, which will have been served last to the group, meaning that most other guests will have finished their main meal by the time the `entertainment' starts. Then the investigator can introduce him- or herself and establish control over the company before coffee is served and surviving group members can circulate around the tables while the guests are drinking the beverage. The remainder of the evening can be spent while the guests are enjoying a post-prandial drink, when they are relaxed and with their appetites satisfied.

Meanwhile, the victim can also relax in the kitchen with his/her cup of coffee! Finally, the victim may or may not, depending on how the producer sees the situation, re-appear brought back to life, perhaps having exposed by his/her apparent death some other dastardly plot...

CASTING

Throughout this book, everything is simply a suggestion as to how an effective murder evening might be given. Every drama group and every producer will be able to think of alternative situations for the dinner, different characters to those suggested in this chapter and other biographies for the characters, to more nearly fit the group that is actually going to put on the entertainment.

The first challenge to be met is 'why is this particular group of people meeting for dinner?' The characters have to be related or (apparently) friends, or, at worst, quite well known to each other.

Although in the expanded casts in subsequent chapters each individual has been blessed with a name, some performers might find it easier to keep their own name for the play (yet another reason to 'play away from home'), unless, of course, they are supposed to be closely related to each other!

Attention should be paid to costume: lapel badges can sometimes tell a story or expand a characterisation and more flamboyant costume can say even more about a character.

In the following 'cast lists' the asterisked individual could well be the 'detective' - though this is yet another area where the final decision is left to individual producers.

In subsequent chapters, the Business Get-together is the only scenario worked out in detail. In the wedding anniversary and the hen party there are some questions that the cast need to have worked out themselves; in Welcome Home there are a few questions that the 'detective' might ask the cast; otherwise you are given suggested biographies and - it's up to you!

Business get-together

Managing Director   M.D.'s wife
Top salesman/woman   M.D.'s secretary
Second ranking salesman Overseas agent
Second ranking salesman's wife
Midland salesman/woman   Company Secretary *
Scottish saleswoman

20th Wedding Anniversary Dinner

Husband   Wife
20 year old son   18 year old daughter
Best Man   Best man's wife
Best man's 18 year old son   Son's girl friend
Husband's unmarried sister   `Grandpa` *

Welcome Home

Man returning from round the world trip
Girl who turned up with him
Mother
Mother's friend *
Younger sister
Newspaper reporter
Best friend, who gave up early on trip
Auntie
Ex-fiancée
Lady from charity benefitting

Getting to know them before the wedding

Father of bride   Mother of bride
Father of groom   Mother of groom
Young clergyman   Sister of bride
Uncle of bride *   Cousin of groom
Cousin of bride   Overseas relation

Leaving party

Girl leaving firm   Her best friend at work
The new office junior *   Sister
Boy friend   His friend
The office gossip   Her friend
The office tea lady   Receptionist

Retirement party

Man retiring from company   His wife
Managing Director   M.D.'s wife
Man taking over job   Man's secretary
Man who hoped to be taking over job
Sales Director   Works manager *
Head of typing pool

Class re-union

Teacher   Ex-students
School handyman

Hen Night

Tomorrow's bride   Matron of honour
Bridesmaid 1   Bridesmaid 2
Girl from shop   Lady who made the cake
Friend from drama   Girl from next door
Friend who moved away   Elder Sister
Policeman *

Engagement party

Boy   Girl
His mother   Her father
His best friend   Her best friend
His sister   Her sister
Her uncle *   Her cousin

Leaving for Australia party

Girl   Mother
Father   Ex-boss
Ex-fiancé   Friend
Sister   Aunt
Australian friend *   Cousin

Society dinner

Chairman   Chairman's wife
Secretary   Secretary's wife
Treasurer   Treasurer's husband
Guest *   Member
Member   Member
Member   Prospective member

Dear old friends

9 people who meet socially every week in a pub have decided to have a meal together.
Policeman *

Youth club dinner

Warden   Warden's wife
Deputy warden   Table tennis champion
Captain of net ball team   Quiz champion
Chairman/woman of Education Committee *
Captain of football team
Head boy of associated school
Head girl of associated school

Running the restaurant

Two bar staff
Wine waiter
'Chef' [not seen until after `accident']
Four waiters/waitresses
Receptionist/Head waiter
Solitary diner (the victim)
Restaurant owner *

BUSINESS GET TOGETHER

Biographies of the group might be on the lines following. It is up to the producer and his cast how much detailed background is sketched in - but, as a rule, the more the better. In embroidering the bare facts below, try to entangle as many of the characters between each other as possible. Is it possible that one of them is the offspring (possibly unknown to any of the others) of another? Is one of the women carrying on with one of the men? Is any one of them working in secret for a rival company? Has one of them got his present job through some sort of skulduggery? The list is endless - and can be funny, if you so desire (as long as feet are kept firmly on the ground and you don't stray into the realms of farce, when the whole evening is liable to collapse around your ears)!

Managing Director
James Smithers. Aged 50. Prosperous.
Has been MD for the past four and a half years, having previously been the company's Sales Director. Before that he had been in charge of overseas sales and had made a number of trips to Europe and North America for the company. He had started with the company as Scottish salesman when he was in his early twenties. Married for eighteen years with a son of 16 and two daughters aged 14 and 13. Lives in a suburb about ten miles from the company's head office and factory.
Was an unexpected choice for MD, as everyone had expected the previous MD's son to take over when he retired - but the son died in a motor accident five and a half years ago. This precipitated the previous MD's retirement and Smithers got the job.
Keen badminton player

Managing Director's wife
Marjorie Smithers. Aged 48. Well presented.
Active in local politics as a Councillor. Energetic organiser of social events for Parent/Teacher Group of the school which all her children attend. Helps in a Charity Shop two mornings a week.
She had been James's secretary before marrying him and had

previously been engaged (for a very short time) to Alan Wont [see below]. She stayed with the company until shortly before the birth of her son and accompanied James on his very first business trip to America. Since then she has not joined him on business trips, mainly because she dislikes flying quite intensely.

She looks forward to holidays with James, generally spent `doing' overseas museums and art galleries (which James detests).

Top salesman/woman

Nicholas (Nicola) Brunt. Aged 35. Dynamic.

Lives for his work. Has been top salesman for the past three years. Has worked for the company four years. Unmarried and, apparently, without any friends of either sex.

Had previously worked for a rival company, but left saying that he could get no further advancement. Is there any-thing in the rumour that he left under some sort of cloud?

Has no sense of humour and little small talk. His conversation is dominated by statistics and sales figures. He is, in fact, the ultimate company bore. Alan Wont was acknowledged top salesman before Nicholas's appearance and very nearly toppled him with sales figures for the past year - but not quite.

Has lived in a series of bed-sits in the past few years, but is usually away on business, staying in hotels around his region.

Managing Director's secretary

Perdita Cassell. Aged 25. Efficient.

Has been with the company six years, all the time as James's secretary, both in his earlier situation and now.

Rumoured to have a boy friend, but keeps her private life away from the office. Within the office is popular and ambitious. Has been enquiring about the chances of taking on a more responsible executive job - personnel is her interest - but James values her too highly to let her go.

Was educated at a girl's school, then `finished' in Switzerland.

Lives in a flat not ten minutes walk from the office, to which she walks each morning.

Second ranking salesman
Alan Wont. Aged 40. Good company.
Has been with the company all his working life, starting as office junior on leaving school. He was office manager before being suddenly switched to sales, for reasons that have never been made public.
Having a friendly manner has done well in sales, but has recently been eclipsed in total figures by Nicholas. Could be that his customers would be more faithful in a crisis, however.
Married to Kathleen, with one daughter aged eleven. Last year another daughter, aged twelve, was killed by a hit and run driver, who has not been detected.
They live in a rather cramped town centre house.
Seems to have little ambition to progress beyond his present job.

His wife
Kathleen. Aged 44. Surprisingly well turned out.
Married for 16 years. Was, before marriage, secretary to James and accompanied him on a number of his European and American trips. Strictly business. An expert on television soaps.
Left the company on marriage and worked in a shop until her daughter was born. Since then she does little outside the house.
But how, one asks, can she have afforded that fur coat - on Alan's salary?

Overseas agent
Clint Smaile. Age 25. Canadian. An eager beaver.
Said to be divorced, though nobody really knows.
Only been with the company for just over a year. This is his first visit to this country, having been engaged by James while he was in Toronto on other business.
Although his territory includes Europe he has never been there and apparently speaks no foreign tongue, except Canadian French. He writes a very persuasive letter however and European sales are marginally up. North American enquiries are booming - though not very much actual business has resulted.
His visit is to acquaint himself with the company's range of products and suggest how they might be better adapted for overseas markets.

Midland salesman
James Threadgold. Age 30. Vigorous.
Been with the company two years. Before that travelled for a company that makes an entirely different sort of product. His territory includes the town where head office and the factory is and he is a familiar face around head office.
An activist in local affairs, upon which he seems to expend a lot of time. Only concerned with his job as far as it brings in enough money for him to pursue his other interests.
Not married, although possessing a reputation for the ladies.
Has been known to drink a little too much on occasion (like the staff Christmas party last year) and recently had a scare that he might lose his driving licence - and therefore his job.

Scottish saleswoman
Andrea McCombie. Age 35. Quiet.
Has been with the company for ten years. Before that had worked in her father's shop (which sold the company's products). Father - and shop - went bankrupt and retiring Scottish rep (now the MD) recommended Andrea to the company. Performs well in an extended territory with little hope for advancement.
Rarely at head office.
A bit of a mystery to head office staff and reticent under questioning: refers to her friend, but whether that friend is male or female is not clear.

Company Secretary
Anthony/Antonia Marshall. Any age. Either sex.
New to company. Comes from town some distance away and is living in a hotel room until he/she finds something more suitable.
Has found the company's books in a slight muddle, though there is no suggestion of any irregularities.

Outstanding questions (among many others) to be decided

What is the company's name?
What does the company manufacture?
What are the names of the various children mentioned?
Where in the political spectrum do Marjorie and James fit?
What was the previous MD's name?
What were Kathleen Wont's and Marjorie Smithers's maiden names?
What school do the Smithers children attend?

The pattern of the evening

The suggested scenario for the evening is that the majority of the group assemble in the bar/foyer at the same time and that they then go in to dinner. One individual might possibly make a late, apologetic, entry.

In the pause between *hors d'oeuvre* and main meal, the MD will rise and, ignoring the other guests in the restaurant (or, maybe, apologising to them in a pleasant fashion), present a trophy or watch or some other suitable recognition to Nicholas for being this year's Top Salesman/woman.

One of the company will choke during dessert and be transported out by the restaurant staff and one of the company; the latter will return and whisper bad tidings to the MD., who seems to go to pieces. The Company Secretary takes over and announces to the other guests that there has been an unfortunate accident to ?, our ?

"Ladies and gentlemen," he/she will then say, skating carefully over the thinnest ice of this part of the evening, "it seems likely that the person who arranged this unfortunate happening is among our party and I would be grateful if you could treat this as confidential until we have sorted out this unpleasantness. My name, by the way, is Anthony/Antonia Marshall and I am the Company Secretary. May I introduce you to the other members of the company sitting around this table."

Basic introductions should then be made. "However, I should tell you that I only joined the company a couple of months ago and so I don't know the background to any of this. Can I suggest that the most sensible way of going on would be for my colleagues to come to each of your tables and tell you something of their background. You can then question them about themselves and their relationships with other people in the company. We want to sort this out as quickly as possible, so I can only give you five minutes per person, after which I will ring this bell. While this is going on I will think up some questions I want to ask and, after I have had my say, there will be the opportunity for you to ask a few supplementary questions."

Individual cast members will then progress round the tables, which have been provided with paper and pencil for their notes.

The first 'five minutes' might be extended slightly to give the cast member a chance to re-explain the pattern of the rest of the evening.

When the course has been completed, the Company Secretary will ask each cast member some questions, varying in number according to the amount of background the character has. The object of this is to bring out various inter-relationships that it is unlikely that the guests on the tables might have asked - even had they been able to guess them. It will stretch the group more if they are 'interviewed' separately with the rest of the group absent.

The questions

For example, the Company Secretary might ask the Managing Director's wife
I believe you are very active in local affairs?
Why do you not accompany your husband on his overseas trips? Does his secretary go with him? Do you approve?
I am told you work in a charity shop a couple of mornings a week. What sort of things do you sell? Has anything unusual been handed in for re-sale recently?
Was James the first and only man in your life?
What do you think of the Borough Council's scheme to re-develop the central area? Will this affect the Wont's house?
Has your husband mentioned to you the rumours that the company is going to be taken over by a Canadian firm?

And remember, unless the MD's wife is the murderer, she has to tell the truth, as far as she knows it. She can, of course, fall back on the

"I don't know", but this should be avoided if possible. So should simple `yes' and `no' answers; unless they see this as part of their character, individuals should try to answer every question as fully as possible. This is where rehearsals prior to the event are shown to be vital!

When the Company Secretary has finished his questions of the MD's wife, there are probably a lot more loose ends lying around than there were before and the paying public is then invited to ask a limited number (say, five or six) of further questions. The MD's wife can then go and have her coffee in peace.

The Company Secretary might ask the Managing Director himself
Do you think the company has been successful under your leadership?
How often do you go abroad these days?
Is that more or less often than when you were Sales Director?
Does your wife accompany you?
There are rumours of a take-over by another company. Is there any truth in this?
Did you know the previous Managing Director's son, who was killed in a motor accident?
The company does not have a Sales Director at present. Was this meeting called for you to assess the potential of the salesmen and women for this post? Will you appoint internally? If so, who?
Where did you go on holiday last year?

Sample questions that might be asked of the Top salesman/woman:
Where is your territory?
You came out as top salesman last year. Has you percentage turnover risen?
Who appointed you to your present job?
What ambitions do you have within the company?
Are you still friends with old colleagues from your previous company?
Is that the company rumoured to be making a take-over of this company?
Do you ever meet any of the people in this evening's group socially?
What do you do in your spare time?
The Sales Director's job is open. If it isn't offered to you, do you

think it should be offered to anyone now within the company?

The overseas agent could be asked:
How did it come about that Mr Smithers offered you your present job?
Are you related to him, or any other members of the company, in any way?
What was your previous job?
Have you ever worked with products manufactured by our company, perhaps with a rival firm?
Have you ever visited head office before?
Can you suggest why so few of your leads result in hard sales?
Are you going to visit the company's depôts in Europe before going back to Canada?

The Midland salesman might be quizzed:
With the benefit of being in Head Office territory, why are your sales figures not better?
Do you ever meet Mrs Smithers in your political activities?
Are you on friendly terms with any of the ladies present this evening?
Perhaps I should have said, are you on intimate terms with any of the ladies?
What are your ambitions, either within the company or politically?
Have you ever visited North America?
Have your drinking habits ever posed a problem?
I wasn't with the company then, but I've heard that there was a scandal after the last company Christmas party. Can you give me details, please?

The second salesman could be posed questions like:
Do you think you might be able to re-gain the top spot in salesmanship next year?
How long have you lived in your present house? Are you thinking of moving?
If you were offered the Sales Directorship, would you take it?
You were once engaged to Marjorie Smithers. What happened?
Why did you switch from being office manager to sales?
Do you think you might do better if you changed jobs to a rival

company?
Were you at the last Christmas party? Is there anything you would like to tell us about it?

The Managing Director's Secretary might be the next to be investigated (although the order is by no means set and can be quite at random):
Do you accompany Mr Smithers on any overseas trips?
Did you go with him to Canada on the occasion that he appointed Mr Smaile to his post?
Do you ever meet other company staff outside office hours?
Are you hoping for promotion within the company?
Is your flat near where the Wont's live?
Have you lived there long?
Do you prepare the statistics on sales for Mr Smithers' examination?
Do you speak any foreign languages?

Kathleen Wont's questions might be something like:
Are you happily married, even though your husband is away most of the week on business?
Do you see any other members of the company's staff socially, ever?
Did you enjoy your business trips with Mr Smithers?
Why did you leave the company when you got married?
Are you friendly with Marjorie Smithers?

The Scottish salesman could be asked:
I am told that your father went bankrupt. Could you give us the details, please?
Do you enjoy working for the company? Do you see any prospects of advancement?
As a proportion of your salary is on commission, do you earn enough to be comfortable?
Do you have any friends in head office?
Do you have any pen pals?
How often do you get down to head office?

Nine sets of questions are here posed, but one of these people will have been the victim - so he/she would not be available for interrogation. The murderer can, if he/she deems it necessary, tell fibs - but has got to remember that he/she might be caught out in an inconsistency by the Company Secretary becaue of someone else's (unscripted, of course) off-the-cuff answers that he/she will not have heard, or the audience.

The motives

A few potential motives are listed, some unlikely, some slightly unbalanced and some for which no allowance has been made in the earlier biographies and/or questions. Some, you will see, are applicable to a number of people.

The Managing Director might have killed
His wife because she is a nag and, frankly, he has hopes for Perdita.
Top salesman because the sales figures have been massaged to make the company more attractive for a take-over, and the Top Salesman knows it!
His secretary because he got her pregnant on their last overseas trip.
The second salesman because he saw the MD fiddling with the previous MD's son's car before the accident and has been blackmailing.
Kathleen Wont because she says she has proof that he was the hit & run driver that killed her daughter.
Overseas agent because he knows about Perdita and that's why he got the job.
Midland salesman because he knows the MD is doing insider dealing with company shares prior to a take-over and is blackmailing.
Scottish saleswoman because she used to be his mistress (when he was Scottish rep) and is now an embarrassment.

The Managing Director's wife might have killed
The Managing Director because he is playing fast and loose with Perdita.
The secretary because of jealousy.
The second salesman because he has threatened to reveal to the

MD that she had a child by him while they were engaged.
Kathleen Wont because she found some of her own clothes in a bundle donated to her charity shop and suspects that the MD is philandering.
Overseas agent because he is the MD's illegitimate son.
Midland salesman because he looks likely to win her Council seat off her at the next election.
Scottish saleswoman because she propositioned her... and that sort of thing is disgusting...

The Top salesman might have killed
The Managing Director because he is impatient of advancement and the old fool is not even going to give his best salesman the Sales director's job!
The MD's wife because she saw him stealing a statuette from an art gallery in Italy while on holiday and has been extorting money from him.
The Secretary because she has twisted the sales figures on his behalf - at a price.
The second salesman because he knows the fiddle the top salesman is indulging in to gain the top place and is content to let him - at a price.
Kathleen Wont because she knows why (through old girl friends) he left his previous job.
Overseas agent because potentially he could topple him as top salesman.
Midland salesman because he saw Top Salesman in head office warehouse doing [what?]

The Managing Director's secretary might have killed
The Managing Director because he has sexually harassed her.
The MD's wife because she is denying the MD his freedom to marry her.
Top salesman because he knows her parents and has threatened to tell them where she is.
Second salesman because is her drug supplier.
Kathleen Wont because she knows she is the hit & run driver.
Overseas agent because he is threatening to tell MD's wife about the goings on during last year's overseas trip.

Midland salesman because he assaulted her at the office Christmas party and she had to have an abortion.
Scottish saleswoman because she arranged the abortion and is threatening to tell all.

The Second Ranking Salesman might have killed
The Managing Director because he is carrying on with his wife.
The MD's wife because he has been carrying on with her and she is threatening to kiss and tell.
The Secretary because she has cooked the sales figures for the past three years in Nicholas' favour.
Top Salesman through frustration and sheer jealousy.
His wife because he rather fancies the Scottish saleswoman.
Overseas agent because he has only been here two weeks and is already suggesting alterations to routines that will make his life less than comfortable.
Midland salesman because he made unwelcome (or were they?) advances to his wife during the office Christmas party, when his wife was drunk-ish.
Scottish saleswoman because she knows the truth about her father's bankruptcy and his part in it.

The Second Ranking Salesman's wife might have killed
The Managing Director because he was the hit & run driver.
The MD's wife because she is Chairman of the Council Committee that plans to redevelop the Town Centre and demolish her cherished home.
Top salesman because he was the hit & run driver.
Her husband because he is carrying on with the MD's Secretary.
The Secretary because she is carrying on with her husband.
Midland salesman because he was the hit & run driver (when drunk).
Scottish saleswoman because she had an affair with her husband when he was Scottish rep.

The Overseas Agent might have killed
The Managing director because he was his (unacknowledged) father.
Top salesman because he knew (somehow) that the OA is a mole in the company on behalf of a large overseas rival.

The Secretary because he fancied her, but she spurned him - and how!
Second ranking salesman because he knew (somehow) that the OA is a mole in the company on behalf of a large overseas rival.
Midland salesman and Scottish saleswoman ditto.

Midland salesman might have killed
Managing Director because he is threatened with dismissal and disgrace because of his drinking - which would scupper his future job prospects and he would have to move.
MD's wife because she is threatening to reveal one of his more horrendous indiscretions to the local newspaper which would finish his political prospects.
The secretary because she was seduced by him at the office Christmas party and is pregnant.
Second ranking salesman because he saw him examining his car and knows he knows that he was the hit & run driver.
Top salesman because he is a capitalist lackey!
Kathleen Wont because she has compromising photographs that would lose him job and local position.
Overseas agent because he has made homosexual advances to him.
Scottish saleswoman because she is pregnant by him.

Scottish saleswoman might have killed
Managing Director because he caused father's bankruptcy.
Top salesman out of sheer envy.
The Secretary because she had refused an offer of a Scottish holiday in no uncertain terms.
Second Salesman because, when he was office manager, he had precipitated her father's bankruptcy.
Midland salesman because he assaulted her at the office Christmas party...

The summation

During rehearsals the biographies and the motives should have been expanded from the outlines suggested here and, consequently, the questions that the Company Secretary can ask should be much more wide ranging - always trying to introduce `red herrings' and suggest new relationships (probably nefarious) between the group.

When all the cast have gone through this examination, the Company Secretary must then submit himself to a few questions from the audience, possibly thrown up by some of the questions he has asked himself and to which he got less-than-satisfactory answers. Being new to the company, of course, the Secretary has an excuse for not answering quite as many leading questions as some of the others.

The Company Secretary then declares the interrogation at an end and passes around the tables with a printed list of the participants' names and invites the guests to decide who is the murderer. As a `tie-break' they are also invited to briefly suggest the motive.

The Company Secretary can spin matters out a little now if he/she wishes by making his own accusations. If he is wrong, the accused can indignantly refute the charge - if he is right, the game is over! In any case, the murderer must now make a clean breast of it and confess and explain why - but then (in this scenario at least) reveal that the poison taken by ? was not fatal, only temporarily paralysing, and the victim can re-appear to present the prize for the winner of the solution.

The person with the hardest task is the Company Secretary, who has to assemble a whole list of questions (most of which should come as a surprise and certainly not be rehearsed with the individual cast members), ranging widely round the characters. He/she should not be shy of making some of them capable of raising laughter, as this has to be an enjoyable evening for the guests - not full of death and destruction.

20TH WEDDING ANNIVERSARY

Husband
William Lather. Aged 43.
Self employed, with five employees. Moderately successful, but a bit paranoid about banks. Very careful with his money.
Used to play rugby in his younger days, and has kept the taste for drinking with his chums. To be found at the local rugby club most Wednesdays and Fridays and has been known to get home slightly under the weather. Other evenings, if he is not balancing his company's books, he will watch television. His work makes him attend some exhibitions around the country from time to time, very occasionally overseas. Regularly takes his wife out for dinner on Saturday evenings: his preference is for Indian meals.

Wife
Hilda Lather, née Speight. Aged 39.
Works as a dentist's receptionist every morning and as her husband's telephonist most afternoons.
Had ambitions to be a 'top' secretary and was working up the ladder when she became pregnant and married William. Still regrets being domesticated quite so suddenly. Had been at school with Trevor Tapping and Patricia 'Trish' Tapping (née Chalkwell) and the four of them are still great friends, going on holidays as a foursome. They used to take the children before they refused to accompany parents any more. Goes to Evening Classes (this year Spanish for beginners, last year Cake decoration) every Monday evening. Has got into the habit of going out on Wednesday and Friday evenings, shortly after William has left out.

20 year old son
Wayne Lather.
Makes a living doing 'this and that', and is always flush with ready cash.
Not to be found at home very often, but returns most evenings rather late just to crash out. Generally still in bed when his parents leave out in the mornings. Left school at the earliest available opportunity,

without scholastic qualifications, although he had been in the school football 1st eleven. Very occasionally has put in a few hours at his dad's factory - when there has been some sort of seasonal rush or staff illness. His parents have no idea who his friends - male or female - are, until now. Has come to this evening's celebrations under heavy protest.

18 year old daughter
Kelly Lather.
Works, uninterestedly, on the till at a local supermarket.
Left school at 16 with good exam results. Would like to be a top model, but has no idea how to go about reaching that goal and little push to get herself there. Obsessed with a current `pop' star and collects everything about him/her. Goes out a lot with her cousin, Denise. Has come to this evening's celebrations under heavy protest.

Best man
Trevor Tapping. Aged 39.
Works in a merchant bank - very successfully. But this means that he is very often not home before bedtime - and is frequently out again the next morning by an early train.
Visits provincial and overseas branches regularly. Has no social outlets, as his times are so erratic, but would like to be concerned with national politics. Married Trish about six months after the Lather wedding. Wants to go somewhere exotic, like the Seychelles, for their next foursome holiday.

Best man's wife
Trish Tapping. Aged 40.
Runs a typing agency from home - for the pin money.
Did some work for the Lather company, but not recently. Now Tim has left home is at a bit of a loose end in the evenings - but is trying various outlets. An excellent cook. The neighbourhood's most notorious gossip! Recently the Lathers and the Tappings have got into the habit of having Sunday lunch at each other's houses alternate weeks.

Best man's son
Timothy Tapping. 18 years old.
Just started university. Very bright.
Was at school with Kelly and Denise. Ambitious to become ? Swims to county standards and trains fanatically. During the last holidays worked for the Lather company temporarily, doing bookkeeping. Few friends and very little social life.

Husband's unmarried sister
Clare Lather. Aged 33.
Recently promoted from being a shop manager to area buyer. Good at many sporting activities. Has had a string of admirers, but has never settled with any of them - to the great annoyance of her sister-in-law. Trevor Tapping has been giving her financial advice recently. Something of a hypochondriac. Active with a local political party.

Son's girl friend
Deborah Smith. Aged 23.
Not the sort you would expect Wayne to have picked up - or vice versa. But she is the first `girl friend' of Wayne's that the Lathers have seen. Timothy knows her - but can't think where from.

`Grandpa'
John Speight. Aged 65.
Retired last month. Widower.
Lives alone, some distance away. Very detached from the rest of the party by age and interests. It happens that this is his 40th wedding anniversary.

A number of questions to be resolved
What does the Lather company do?
A number of people have worked for the Lather company: do they know anything discreditable?
How does Wayne make his living?
Is Deborah a `genuine' girl friend?
Where does Deborah work - or say she works?
What does Hilda do on her evenings out?
Where has Trish landed up on her new evenings out?
What is Timothy studying?

Where do Kelly and Denise spend their time?
Is there more to Kelly than there appears?
What products does Clare deal in? Might her shops buy from the Lather company?
Is Trevor <u>always</u> working late at the office?
What did John retire from?

These, and many more, can be either incorporated into the biographies or can be brought out by the interrogator - who will probably be 'Grandpa', but could conceivably be Deborah (if she turns out to be an undercover policewoman!).

Motives... questions to be asked... up to you!

Welcome Home

Returning 'hero'
David Spaul. Aged 26.
Has been away for the past two years, cycling around the world, supporting himself by casual work. Had previously worked as a lowly Civil Servant. Has sent very few informative letters home during his trip, but postcards from a number of places. Doesn't look very weatherbeaten, but he claims this is because he has been working in a restaurant kitchen in New York for the past three months getting the money to get back across the Atlantic. Arrived home virtually unannounced six days ago.

The Girl Friend
Claudia Sampidoro. Aged 24.
Italian. Met David in America. Very glamorous; did bit parts in television commercials in USA and hopes to break into British television. Says that Daddy is funding her visit to Britain, but she is anxious to find work to support herself. Has been staying in the spare room at the Spauls since arriving in Britain with David. She is expected to return home to Sicily for at least a visit before she returns to America.

Mother
Rita Spaul. Aged 55.
A very dominant personality: how David managed to fly from the nest we might find out. Has worked in a local supermarket check-out for the past eighteen months. Widow. Her husband died shortly after David had gone away and she wasn't able to let him know. Before marriage was a cashier in a local bank, but was then a housewife for 28 years. Her only interests are in the home. Has never been further away than Brighton on holiday.

Mother's friend
John Tayler. Aged 60.
Retired policeman (where latterly, he was a dog-handler), now doing a part-time job delivering cars from distributors to show-rooms.

Widower, who got to know Rita in supermarket, when she helped him with advice on cooking about six months ago. Still a member of the Police Choir, which sang in their `twin town' in France last month. When a young man played professional football for an obscure team for one season only. Has not previously met David.

Younger sister
Mary Spaul. Aged 23.
Engaged to be married to Mike. Works in a local bank doing foreign exchange. Would love to travel, but has been forbidden by Mother "until David comes home". Enjoys disco dancing at a local pub; not at all a domesticated young lady.

Newspaper reporter
Wendy Connor. Aged 26.
Knew David (since junior schooldays) before he travelled. A voluminous letter-writer with world-wide `pen pals' . Now collecting data for interview that she hopes might sell to a national newspaper, as well as her local `rag'. Visited Rome on holiday last summer.

Best Friend
Mike Johns. Aged 26.
Set off with David, but gave up after one month, at which time they had reached Naples, for reasons he has not specified. Works in local garage. Engaged to Mary for the past four months: marriage a distant prospect, because of his financial position. Amateur sportsman.

Auntie
Anne Applebee. Aged 60+
Not a real Aunt, but has lived next door to the Spauls for years. A gossip of the first water. Her husband works at the local railway station, and is on duty tonight. Works part-time in a local charity shop. The Applebees go in for (free) rail travel holidays and are planning a trip to Switzerland or beyond next year.

Ex-fiancée
Beth Armstrong. Aged 24.
Works for a local veterinarian. Agreed that it would be sensible for both of them to `break it off' when David went abroad. Currently unattached. Keen on volleyball, hockey and swimming.

Lady from charity
Penelope Masters. Aged 30.
Expecting to (eventually) receive cheque from David for sponsored ride. Works for charity voluntarily and is Deputy Manager of supermarket (where Rita works) in full-time occupation. Is very keen on helping the under-privileged of this world. A fanatic cat owner.

Questions that Auntie might ask include
Of David
Do you like Australia/India/America/Canada/wherever?
Under what circumstances did you meet Claudia?
Which restaurant did you do your washing up job in?
Have you met Claudia's family?
Why did Mike abandon the cycle trip - and where?
To finance your trip where else, apart from New York, did you work? Doing what?
Knowing your Mum would have liked to know more about where you were, why didn't you write long letters home?
Have you seen Beth since you came home - before this evening?
Why did you select Mrs Masters' charity for your sponsorship?

Of Claudia
Under what circumstances did you meet David?
Given that David was working most evenings, how did you get further acquainted?
What does your family think of your coming here with David?
Had you previously met or corresponded with any other people here this evening - apart from David, of course?
How regular is your work on television?
How big an allowance has your father given you for this trip?

Of Mother
How was it that you let David leave on his trip?
Why wouldn't you let Mary `off the leash'?
At anytime had you any idea where David might be?
Did you know that he was working in New York?
Did you know he was going to bring Claudia here?
Do you approve of Mary's friendship with Mike?

Of John Tayler
Do you have any contacts with police in other countries?
I understand you went abroad recently; have you ever been to Italy?
When you were a dog-handler, did you ever meet Miss Armstrong professionally?
How do you see your friendship with Rita developing?

Of Mary
Were you working in the foreign exchange section of your bank when David left on his trip?
Do you expect to marry Mike?
What have you and he in common?
Do you still live at home with your Mother?
Have you any views on your mother's friendship with Mr Tayler?

Of Wendy
Where do you have `pen pals'?
Have any of them mentioned that David has been in their vicinity?
When in Italy last year did you meet any of the Sampidoro family?
In your interviews with David for your newspaper articles, has anything strange struck you about his travels?

Of Mike
Why did you give up the cycle ride with David?
How did you get home from Naples then?
How long have you been engaged to Mary?
Have you been interviewed for her articles by Wendy?
When you were in Italy did you meet the Sampidoro family?
A month is a long time to get to Naples; did you do any work to raise funds in that month?

Of Beth
Just between ourselves, do you still like David? Enough to marry him?
Are you jealous of Claudia?
You swim for the local club. Is Mike also a member of the team?
Did David write to you while he was away?
Do you every go disco dancing?

Of Penelope Masters
Why do you think David chose your charity to sponsor?
Does your charity have any connections with Italy?
Have you every taken your cats to Miss Armstrong for medication?
Is Mrs Spaul a good employee?
Is it coincidence that Mrs Spaul works in your supermarket or did you first meet her when David approached your charity?

The purpose of the questions, of course, is to work up any Mafia links between the characters and to try to establish that there are previous connections - possibly suspicious. Can a young lady in a bank launder money...? Could a dog-handler's dog have sniffed out drugs...? Did David make homosexual advances to Mike on the trip...? Did David or Mike or Wendy or Claudia carry drugs - and did anyone guess this? And so on, and so on...

GETTING TO KNOW THEM

Father of the bride
John Lockyer. Aged 55
Sales manager with large company. In the summer he gardens in the grounds of his large house; in the winter he collects stamps: specialises in stamps about plants. His company has branches in Britain and USA, so he frequently has to leave home for the odd ten days or so. Not popular at work because of wandering hands

Mother of the bride
Cynthia Lockyer (née Douglas). Aged 43
Housewife. Member of a variety of church organisations, and sometimes helps in a church 'soup kitchen' that regularly visits 'down and outs' in nearby town. Would love to accompany John on his travels - but is never asked! The Lockyers have two other younger daughters. Obsessive about her weight and almost lives with a calorie chart in her hands A teetotaller, is not reconciled to her brother running a pub

Father of the groom
Charles Askew. Aged 48
Buyer for a department store. The Askews live in a flat. In his spare time he writes crime novels. Has had four published, and has hopes of a further three that are waiting publishers' decisions.
At weekends and on holiday he goes around looking for 'copy'. Often to be found scribbling stories in the public gallery of the local police court

Mother of the groom
Amabel Askew (née Warwick). Aged 50
Teacher of English and history at local school. In her spare time she also writes, mostly biographies. Has had a number of books published under a pseudonym. Normally holidays apart from Charles, as she spends most of her spare time in libraries researching. Currently researching a recently-deceased local notability. The Askews have one younger daughter.

Sister of the bride
Pauline Lockyer. Aged 19
Works in Askew's department store, in the stock rooms. Very good artist - "should have taken it up as a career". Has just `broken up' with boy friend. Introduced the groom to her sister some six months ago when she had been taken by the groom to a disco. A reputation as a `bit of a flirt'.

Sister of the groom
Sarah Askew. Aged 20
Student teacher, aiming to teach English and drama, when she qualifies next year. Before she went away to college was a member of church choir. At college she is living with two other students. Home for the vacation - but intends to join a pony trekking holiday immediately after the wedding.

Cousin of the bride
Samantha Lockyer. Aged 29
John's elder brother's daughter. The family live near and are constant visitors (Her parents cannot be here because they are not due back from holiday until tomorrow - the wedding day). Wanted to go on the stage, but was too tall. Is school secretary where Amabel works. Teaches classical ballet in her spare time.

Cousin of the groom
Raymond Mitchell. Aged 22
Amabel's elder sister's son. In the army, on leave. When he leaves the army wants to be a chef. Used to go to school with the bride, and was romantically linked to her by school friends' gossip. His parents not present because of a family row. He doesn't care that he'll be in the dog-house for coming this evening.

Uncle of the bride
Michael Douglas. Aged 38
Publican. His wife is looking after the bar tonight and she will attend the wedding tomorrow, while he stays in the pub. No children. His establishment has a rather dubious reputation as many local `villains' seem to meet there. The bride used to help part-time in pub in evenings - but left about a year ago.

Clergyman
Austin Carter. Aged 26
This is going to be his first wedding. A local boy (and a bit of a tearaway!) before entering the church; now returned to his own patch after theological college and ordination. His identical twin brother works in Askew's department store as a window dresser

POSSIBLE MOTIVES

The father of the bride might want to kill
His wife because she has found out what he does abroad
Mr Askew because he has snooped out a Lockyer secret
Mrs Askew because she is absolutely certain that Lockyer raped her younger daughter and threatens to make a public announcement in church tomorrow
Miss Askew because she is blackmailing him about the rape
Raymond because he is the father of the bride's (unannounced) pregnancy
Douglas because he knows Lockyer grows cannabis in his garden and is threatening to tell the police
Revd Carter because they had a homosexual relationship before Carter 'saw the light'.

The mother of the bride might want to kill
Her husband because he had an incestuous relationship with the bride
Mr Askew because he has found out that the soup kitchen sells drugs
Mrs Askew because she is blackmailing Cynthia, having found out the truth about her parents (!)
Samantha because she has been living with the groom
Raymond because he has found that the soup kitchen is really a thieves' kitchen
Douglas because he had introduced the bride into a financial scam while she was working at the pub

The father of the groom might want to kill
Mr Lockyer because Lockyer is the brains behind a take-over bid that will put Charles out of work
Mrs Lockyer because she has found out that he has lifted all his books from foreign authors, altering the setting, and is threatening to expose him
His wife because she has caught him doing 'research' with a local prostitute
Pauline because she has found about his sideline at his department store
Samantha because she is an amateur prostitute and has given him a socially unacceptable disease
Raymond because he is the reason for the family row
Douglas because he had been meeting local villains at the pub: now he might be unmasked
Carter because he thinks that the reverend gentleman is the window-dresser in 'disguise' - and the window dresser is blackmailing him...

The mother of the bride might want to kill
Mr Lockyer because he seduced her when she was a girl and this is the first time she has seen him since then
Mrs Lockyer because Mrs Lockyer is a local brothel keeper and has enveigled her younger daughter into the net
Her husband because ...
and so on... and so on.
The motives do not have to be logical among each other, as each will have to stand on its own.
Motives are generally either sexual or financial. Jealousy might enter if the murderer is slightly unbalanced.

LEAVING PARTY

The girl leaving the firm
Peggy Nash. Aged 25
Has worked with the company since she left school. Has risen to become Sales Manager's Personal Assistant. Was offered and is taking job as Assistant Sales manager at rival company. Attends art classes, but is not a very good artist. Popular - but very quick tempered. Has turned down three offers of marriage from and refuses to live with Michael.

Her boy friend
Michael Prince. Aged 27
Assistant Sales Manager at company for past three years. Promoted to that post after coming to management attention as Trade Union rep for the factory floor. Probably at the limit of his abilities. Fed up with being dominated by and refused by Peggy.

Her best friend at work
Susan Armitage. Aged 23
The star of the typing pool. Has no ambition within the company, regarding it as a social place where she can discuss boy friends, dances, last night's TV, tennis (or whatever has her attention at the moment). No permanent boy friend of her own - apparently. Good at mathematics; types the company's accounts

Her sister
June Nash. Aged 23
Lives with her fiancé, who is a clerk at the rival company. She works as a home help, usually for short periods with people convalescing from hospital. Has been on a numbering of catering courses and would like to take it up professionally.

The office gossip
Sharon Meadows. Aged 26
The Managing Director's Personal Assistant. Knows everybody and everything that happens - or might have happened. Not above

starting a rumour and then reporting it as truth when it 'gets back' to her. It is said that she is out to win the Managing Director, who is married to a career-woman Head Teacher.

The tea lady
Dorothy Scales. Aged 40-ish
A 'non-gossip', always pretending that she knows 'something' about someone. What she does know is more about the company than some of its directors, as she is ignored by people discussing important matters, as she delivers refreshments. Doubles as First Aid Nurse for the staff.

Boy friend's friend
Rodney Bourne. Aged 26
Dragged along so that Michael will not be the only man in the party. Knows most of the people at dinner, having met them casually socially. A salesman in a car firm. Very assured.

Boy friend's girl friend
Mavis Nellis. Aged 18
Thinks Rodney is marvellous; met him at a dance three months ago and has just moved in with him - against her parents' express wishes. A shop assistant. Likes dancing, football... and Rodney.

Receptionist
Gloria Speller. Aged 23
An unashamed listener on her switchboard, but keeps herself to herself. Aware that there is a chance of the company being taken over by its rival. Has worked for the company for three years. No known boy friends. At school was an Olympic hope at swimming - but retired when she was 16.

New office junior
Janet Briggs. Aged 18
Very keen; willing to do anything for anybody - but wants to know the reasons for her work. Has become friendly with Peggy because she also wants to work in Sales and has worked in that department most of the previous eight weeks, after 'filling in' at various of the company office departments.

RETIREMENT PARTY

Man retiring
Walter Scudamore
Aged 61, taking early retirement, after a mild heart attack six months ago. He has not been at work since then. Was the Company Secretary/Accountant. A keen gardener, his present is something to do with gardening. He has been with the company for the past thirty years. Would like to retire to `somewhere sunny', but his wife doesn't want to move.

His wife
Helen Scudamore, née Johnson.
Age 58.
Married 38 years. Housewife. Three children, all grown-up and all moved some distance away. Proud of two grandchildren (with another on the way) and looking forward to seeing more of them in future. Her main interest is playing bridge, which she does three afternoons a week. Walter is not interested. She tries to visit neighbouring towns at least once a week and there she haunts junk shops, auction sales and car boot sales. Thinks she has an eye for a `bargain'.

Managing Director
Philip Jenkinson.
Aged 43.
Appointed to post only twelve months ago. A `Company man' with limited interests outside his work. Has shaken the firm up since he got there, sacking a number of administrative staff, but appointing more people `on the road'. Used to work as an accountant in a rival firm (in neighbouring town), but was `head hunted' by company Chairman. Newly elected to local Chamber of Commerce & Industry. National Officer for his professional association.

Managing Director's Wife
Bunty Jenkinson, formerly Boran, née Richards.
Aged 33 - but admits to 26.
Philip's second wife. They met on a holiday in Greece three years ago and were `mutually attracted' - two divorces resulted. Dislikes her new house and new town and compares them unfavourably with previous home and town. Has no intention of spoiling her figure by having children. Spends a lot of time and money at her hairdressers. Her main relaxation is going to the nearby large city to go to the theatre: has recently been coming home rather late as she is making a habit of eating after the performance - she says.

Man taking over job
Richard Charles.
Aged 35.
Used to work for Philip in previous company. Has been working in job for past three months (when it became clear that Walter would not be coming back). Still living in lodgings, but looking for flat. Separated from wife, with 2 children whom he sees weekly. An expert ski-er in the winter and swimmer in the summer. Goes away for a considerable number of `long weekends'. His annual leave entitlement is unknown to Cedric Holmes (who is prepared to resent any arrangement).

Man who hoped to take over job
Cedric Holmes.
Aged 48.
Walter's deputy (and now Richard's) for the past twelve years. Looking desperately for another job - anywhere - anything. Married with three children. His wife enjoys poor health; she should have been here this evening, but has a migraine and has cancelled at last minute. Secretary of local Rotary. Social Secretary of local PTA, although all his children have left school. Enthusiastic member of the local historical society

Man's Secretary
Adrienne Porlock.
Aged 25.
Has worked for company since leaving school. Walter's (now Richard's) secretary for past three years. Doesn't like Richard as well as Walter. Looking vaguely for another job. Lives with parents, but is looking (also vaguely) for her own place. No (known) boy friends. Is a member of St John's Ambulance Brigade and often attends local theatres in that capacity

Head of typing pool
Marsha Boston.
Aged 35.
An agressive feminist. Would like to get a job in personnel - not necessarily with this company. Honorary Secretary to local Chamber of Commerce & Industry. Lives in nearby town, alone (?) Drives to work in very flashy roadster (which is a company joke, not appreciated by Marsha).

Works Manager
Tony Smith
Aged 40.
Regards everyone in an office job as not really working. Has been with company since leaving school, working up from apprentice. Has been Captain of works football team for years. Will only give up if he thinks a suitable replacement has come along - an unlikely prospect! Lives alone on smallholding on town outskirts, where he grows most of his own vegetables, brews his own beer, keeps bees, small orchard. The most anti-social of men, he has been dragged along to this dinner because Jenkinson insisted.

CLASS REUNION

With this one, you're very much on your own!
You have to decide whether it has been an adult class with mixed ages/sexes or a school class perhaps meeting five/ten/twenty years after they have left school, what subject has been taught or if it was an examination class, how many times a week they used to meet...
It can probably be assumed that the teacher is older than his/her pupils, but, of course, if it was an adult class, this is not essential.
The pupils may be of an age - have they dramatically different backgrounds? Did some of them, for example, go to university, leaving others behind in the town. Have some of them moved away after school, now returning for a special visit?
If they were studying one specific subject have any of them advanced beyond the teacher's capacity - at university or abroad, maybe?
You may wonder why the school handyman (caretaker?) has been invited. Obviously he was a popular figure. Why?
Whatever happens, they are heading for a dramatic moment later in the evening, so their lives must be entangled in a number of ways - or perhaps entangled with an individual or individuals who are, significantly, not here this evening.
Good luck!

HEN PARTY

Tomorrow's bride
Susan Armitage. Age 25.
Has been living with John Smith for two years. Announced wedding quite suddenly six weeks ago. Works in bakers and confectioners shop. Has been in the Winter Amateur Thespians for six years or so, generally playing maids and other minor parts. Passed her driving test last week. Has said quite openly that she wants to leave 'this boring town' as soon as John can find another job - perhaps overseas

Bridesmaid one
Penny Strong. Age 25.
Has known Susan since school. Works as receptionist in taxi company. Was briefly engaged to John when she was 21, but broke it off when he wanted her to move in with him. In local church choir. Lives with Bridesmaid 2 in small flat

Bridesmaid two
Sharon Locke. Age 24.
Has known Susan since school. In local council, doing the hall bookings and other similar. Was in drama group for short time, but left to join a rival company. Has been 'going steady' with Alan Drake since they were at senior school together.

Matron of honour
Linda Long, née Locke. Age 26.
Has known Susan since school. Married with eighteen-month-old boy. Used to work for council before marrying Charles Long, with a senor position in the Borough Treasurer's, some twenty years older than her. Before her marriage was regarded as a bit flighty. Penny, Sharon and Susan often baby-sit for her. Her father, although a couple of years older than Charles, works under him in the Council offices

Girl from next door
Alexa Danbury. Age 22.
Student at College to be a primary school teacher. Is at college with John's brother, Kevin. Has only lived next door for two years, before then lived in town where Samantha now resides

Elder sister
Elizabeth Armitage. Age 28.
Still at parents' home. Peripatetic music teacher in local schools. Has obliged by playing piano for WAT from time to time. Hypochondriac. Avid reader of romantic novels

Friend who moved away
Samantha Neal. Aged 25.
Has known Susan since school. Parents still live in town, but Samantha moved to town some fifty miles away three years ago. Is employed as a sales rep and often returns to home town. When she needs to stay overnight, she `borrows' a bed from Penny and Sharon, refusing to see her parents.

Girl from shop
Lucilla Benge. Aged 20.
Has worked with Susan for the past three years. Had been very bright at school and could have gone to university - but didn't. Is a little pregnant.

Girl from drama
Melanie Scott. Aged 23.
Has been in drama group for past four years and has had the `lead' in plays for the past couple of years. Is unemployed, but doesn't seem to either care or be hard up. Lives alone in local Council flat - though how she got it...?

Policewoman
June Thomas. Aged 29.
Has been in the police for five years and is hoping for promotion very soon. Knows Susan Armitage from being the local `beat' policeman in the area around her shop. Knew the Smith brothers when they were very young, living in town a short distance away.

Questions

Is John Smith in the drama group?
What does John Smith do for a living?
How old is John Smith?
Where is the wedding to be held?
Who is the father of Lucilla's child?
Why did Sharon leave drama group?
What does Samantha travel in?
How does Melanie survive financially?
Did Alexa and Samantha meet when the latter moved away?
Does Susan resent Melanie getting the peach parts?
Was Linda's baby fathered by Charles?
Why is Lucilla in a dead-end job?
Does June know anything to the detriment of the Smiths?
Why won't Samantha return home?

Expand the biographies and the questions keep coming. Not all the questions are worth asking. Not all are relevant to the matter in hand - but there are a whole host of other questions that do exist.

THE ENGAGEMENT PARTY

Boy
Neil McDonald. Aged 22
Clerk in a local bank, where he met Emma. Ambitious; thinks that to have a wife would be good for his future image. Active socially, but only because he thinks that he should be. Bitterly regrets not having been able to go to university. Wants children - a boy and a girl - because that is the ideal family for a Bank Manager.

Girl
Emma Curton. Aged 21
A teller at the bank. Would like to get married in a couple of years' time - and is already planning the wedding, the honeymoon and their little home, in fine detail. Not at all sure about wanting children. Enjoys going on long walking weekends with girl friends

His mother
Anne McDonald. Aged 46
Has been widowed for three years, after a car accident in which she was also injured quite badly. Has lived in the town all her life. Makes `ends meet' by doing needlework for a select band of neighbours. Devoted to her son: Emma is `not good enough' for him! When Neil leaves home, she says she will move...

Her father
Norman Curton. Aged 47
Divorced for five years, his ex-wife accusing him of adultery with a (now no longer in town) much younger woman. Wealthy, owns a furniture removal company. Prepared to do anything for money. Knows his law and is prepared to bend it to his own advantage. Prominent member of Rotary, which runs the local Carnival. On the Committee of local Chamber of Commerce.

His best friend
Timothy Reed. Aged 22
At school with Neil, but now at University in his final year. A

scientist, he fully expects to get a job that takes him away from the town and into the large world. Has a steady girl friend at University, but she refuses to come to the town with him - for unexplained reasons. In the University Athletics team.

Her best friend
Samantha Cockerton. Aged 21
Has known Emma since they were babies. Lives next door to the Curtons. Works as in accounts in the Curton removal business. Romantically linked with Timothy when they were 16 or so. No regular boy friends now. A member of the local Harriers. Carnival Queen last year. Has recently been complaining of feeling unwell.

His sister
Lynn McDonald. Aged 20
Works in local library, but is looking forward to going away to Library School next year. Has a multiplicity of boy friends. Does not like Emma. Won prizes at school for her chemistry.

Her sister
Helen Curton. Aged 18
Bitterly regrets not living with her mother after the divorce. In her last year at 6th Form College, hoping for University place, where she would study law - she thinks. A very serious young lady, who has rarely gone out socially - let alone with boys!

Her cousin
Margaret Scott. Aged 24
Works as a clerk in the local Police Station. To be married in a few weeks' time to a local policeman. They will be setting up home in a (free) police house. Prize-winning amateur potter.

Her father
Jim Scott. Aged 46
A self-employed plumber. His wife 'disappeared' four years ago while visiting a relative some distance away. It was not immediately realised that she was missing and police investigations did not begin until she had been gone for about 4 weeks. 'POLICE BAFFLED' - local newspaper headline.

LEAVING FOR AUSTRALIA PARTY

The girl
Joan Reddish. Aged 24
Qualified dental nurse. Has worked for Frank Scott for twelve months. Was deeply hurt when Robert broke off their engagement. Has been offered a job in Melbourne. Has never previously been abroad. Flies away the day after tomorrow.

Mother
Irene Reddish (née Starling). Aged 54
A doctor in a group practice in the town. Does voluntary work in the slums in the nearby university city. Very out-going. Her father, before he retired, was leader of the group practice. A golf widow, she then took up the game herself.

Father
Ashley Reddish. Aged 55
The Librarian of the University Medical Library. Belongs to the International Society of Medical Librarians. Failed to complete his medical training and turned to librarianship. Has written a standard textbook on classification of medical libraries. Deeply academic with few outside interests, except golf which he plays almost to excess.

Sister
Lindsey Reddish. Aged 26
Has just qualified as a doctor, but has not yet found a post. At medical school she met Arthur Coke, but has not yet told her parents she proposes to live with him - in a distant town. Her training was at (another) university, so she has not lived at home for some five years: just during vacations.

The ex-boss
Frank Scott. Aged 28
Dentist. Qualified three years ago and bought an old-established dental practice some eighteen months ago. Trained at the same medical university as Lindsey, although starting a couple of years

before her. Originally lived in the poorer part of the nearby university city and has clawed his way up by sheer ability.

Ex-fiancé
Robert Thurmarsh. Aged 26
Son of a local builder, he does the estimating for his father's (prosperous) firm. Met Joan at a demonstration, when people were protesting about his father demolishing an old building in the town for redevelopment. Joan was slightly hurt in a scuffle and Robert took her to hospital; the friendship blossomed into engagement a year ago. He broke the relationship off with no explanation six months later and has avoided her since. Was invited to dinner unexpectedly (as far as he was concerned) and, in the circumstances, felt he could not be 'rude' and stay away.

Friend
Rosemary Percival. Aged 24
Works in a local travel agency. Has known Joan since they were at Infants' School together. She and her friend, Tim Geary, made up the regular four-some with Joan and Robert for dances, meals out and other entertainment. Since their break-up, has not seen a lot of Joan. An enthusiastic ten-pin bowler. Recently selected as a 'no hope' candidate in a local Council by-election.

Aunt
Cynthia Starling. Aged 40
Lecturer in anatomy at university. Not married, but romance has been rumoured from time to time. Lives in town in a house on the new Thurmarsh Estate: previously resided in the building knocked down by Thurmarsh Senior. Keen yachtswoman.

Cousin
Mary Reddish. Aged 21
Daughter of Ashley's younger brother, Austin. Works in the laboratory of a local pharmaceutical manufacturer. Her father and uncle are not very close and she has only been invited this evening because her parents are attending a conference in India and she is alone at their home, also on the Thurmarsh Estate.

Australian friend
Sheila Krojanski. Aged 25
Also a dental nurse, attending the same course as Joan. Since qualifying has not looked for a permanent job, as she has been on `walk-abouts' for extended holidays in Europe. Has worked temporarily for both Thurmarsh Estates, Ltd., and the pharmaceutical company, so she knows Robert and Mary, as well as Joan's immediate family. Returning to Australia with Joan, but she will be going to Adelaide, where she has no job lined up.

SOCIETY DINNER

The Chairman
Sebastian ('Bill' to his friends)Bridge. Aged 53
Works for the police in a civilian job. Has been Chairman of this Society that has international connections, for the past three years. During his Chairmanship there have been a number of new, influential members introduced - after a number of years of stagnation. Expects to travel abroad on Society business four or five times a year. Lives in a luxury apartment in a new block of flats. Active in charity work for various local organisations.

The Chairman's wife
Doreen Bridge. Aged 46
Before marrying Sebastian (known to her as 'Sebastian') six years ago was a hairdresser. Slightly over-awed by Sebastian's influential friends and only rarely accompanies him on his trips. Helps with the local charity work, usually in a menial capacity. Is bored out of her mind in the flat.

The Secretary
Giles Waterhouse. Aged 45
An eager beaver, who does most of the Society's work and correspondence, but only gets invited to a few of the Society's international functions. Garage proprietor in 'real' life. Freemason. Prominent supporter of local youth services. Friend to all, often inviting 'strays' home unexpected by his wife - very occasionally regretting it afterwards!

The Secretary's wife
Mavis Waterhouse. Aged 42
Very house-proud. In the garden a fallen leaf can only expect to lie on the lawn for five minutes before being composted! Is appalled at Giles' habit of inviting unknowns home: some of them are untidy and, a couple of times, things have gone missing afterwards! Has been married twenty years, later this year. No children - messy things!

The Treasurer
John Dobbs. Aged 55
Chartered accountant, who volunteered to check the Society's books about seven years ago. Rumoured that his employers are heading for bankruptcy. A very private person - with unexpected flashes of flair.

The Treasurer's wife
Veronique Dobbs. Aged 25
Dobbs' second wife, whom he met while abroad on Society business. Heavily expectant and baby-obsessed. Still trying to learn local customs. Very conscious that she is the second Mrs Dobbs (although she has not met the first). Enjoying living in a large house.

Prospective member
Richard Simmonds. Aged 40
Local bank manager. Banks for most local charities. Has been acquainted with the Society for some years, but is only now being invited to join; there is an initiation ceremony which he does not know about! Has travelled extensively. Is a judge at various dog shows across the country.

Prospective member's wife
Vanessa Simmonds. Aged 45
Chartered accountant in private practice, on the Investigations Panel of her Institute. Suspicious of the Society, which seems to her to be very male-orientated. The Simmonds have one son, at university abroad. Recently de-selected from the Ladies' County Golf Team and now determined to get her game up to scratch again. Audits the books for a local hospice and for various other smaller charities.

Guest
Janet Summers. Aged 45
Chairman of Finance in the local Council. Although not eligible to join the Society (being female), there is a tradition of inviting influential people to the dinner. In private life is friends with the Simmonds. A widow in comfortable circumstances, although her late husband was simply a taxi driver. Has recently moved to one of the larger houses in town.

Member
William Carter. Aged 62
Retired office manager. Has been in the Society for twenty years, without ever taking a leading rôle. Multi-lingual and beginning research to write a history of the Society, using material from many countries. A recent widower, with three adult children. Has consistently `black-balled' Richard Simmonds from becoming a member of the Society, but has this year withdrawn all opposition.

Member
James Sands. Aged 48
The newest member of this branch of the Society. A pilot in a small aircraft company, specialising in business flights. Divorced about three years ago. In the process of selling his house. His mother recently died in the local hospice. His only daughter works voluntarily in a local charity shop. His elder son has just signed forms to become a professional footballer. His younger son is still at school and living with his ex-wife.

DEAR OLD FRIENDS

Their only obvious connection is that they all meet regularly socially and chat amongst themselves and, maybe, play games available in their meeting place - pool, darts, cribbage, shove ha'penny, bowling, etc.

Beneath the surface, we don't know - yet - whether any of them meet outside the weekly meeting; or if one or more of them is using the group as a cover for passing material on to another individual; or if any of them knew any of the others before these regular meetings began.

We don't know what the balance of sexes is, although we may guess that they are probably more or less of an age.

One of them will have arranged this evening's dinner and, for one reason or another, a couple of them will have been reluctant to come - but are here because of peer pressure.

They will all be drinkers - but moderate. Regular drinkers generally pace their consumption over an evening.

Maybe the Policeman, who will have to sort out all the unpleasantness, is also a regular of the group - but he might not be quite so regular, because of his job's hours. It could be that another of the group is not such a regular attender for reasons we might find out: maybe he/she flashes money around a little bit more than likely and is less known to the others.

Each of them will harbour various guilty associations (perhaps only in their minds) with most of the others.

Of course, they might be regulars at the pub either for the entire evening or just after some other diversion - evening class, rehearsal, art group, etc.

The combinations are endless - over to you...

YOUTH CLUB DINNER

Warden
Charles Slocombe. Aged 45-55
Runs the Club in his spare time, full-time job is with an insurance company. Has been at the Club for over ten years, bringing it up from being a 'sink' club, to being well-regarded both by its members and the authorities. The club has some 200 members and runs a number of teams in a number of sports. Likes things to be 'just so'. Married eight years ago. No children. Regards the Club members as his 'babies'. Has known John Newton and his wife since before they were married. Intensely proud of the Club garden, in which he has spent a lot of time: two weeks ago it was extensively vandalised.

Warden's wife
Anna Slocombe. Aged 50-60
Born in Germany. Met Charles about 10 years ago, when he was visiting Twin Town. A bit of a mystery to Club members; said by them to have lived in a castle in Germany and to be a Grand Duchess in her own right. Often helps out in the club 'bar'. Does occasional work as translator for local companies either for correspondence or to help visitors. The Slocombes live in a town centre flat, some distance from the Club.

Deputy Warden
Wayne Bolt. Aged 30-ish
Unemployed and spends a lot of his time at the Club, doing odd jobs and opening it when teams need to play outside 'normal' hours. Used to work in a sports goods shop, but was accused of theft from the till: spent twelve months in prison as a result. Popular with Club members; Charles thinks too popular. Is currently organising a tour for the football team and another for the netball team.

Head girl of school
Elaine Smith. Aged 17
Member of Club, where she is Deputy Captain of Netball, but Mother will probably not let her go on the tour. Tipped for University, widely expected to do well in exams. Lives near school where Club has its premises. Her mother insists that she is home by 10 o'clock - except on special occasions (like tonight). Jazz enthusiast

Head boy of school
John Carr. Aged 18
Not a Club member. Academic; hopes to be a doctor. His father is a teacher at the school. School chess champion and Head of Debating Society (they won a Rotary prize against all local schools only last week). Has taken Maggy to cinema a couple of times - and to the school dances.

Captain of netball
Maggy Warlock. Aged 16
Good at most types of athletics: has represented school and Club at County level - and is expected to improve. Spends as much time at Club as she possibly can - to the detriment of her school work (think her parents). Thinks John `rather super' and has pushed herself on him.

Quiz champion
Kelly Morgan. Aged 18
Has left school, but has not yet found a job. Possibly going to college next term. Has helped re-paint the club house with Wayne. Has ambitions to work for local radio station. Lives in a house backing on to school. Both inquisitive and a gossip. Rich father has just bought her a car.

Chairman of Education Committee
Peter Newton. Aged 40-ish
Councillor of some nine years standing, but only recently appointed as boss of Education. This is his first official meeting with Club members, although he knows some of them because of Civic duties. His wife never accompanies him on this sort of occasion; rumoured she is a secret solitary drinker. Is a Governor of the school. Has two

children at the school; one of them is also a member of the Club and in the junior football team. In private life he is the accountant in a sports wear manufacturer. Member of Round Table.

Table Tennis Champion
Monica Holmes. Aged 15

Although she lifted the Cup against fierce competition, has not played seriously since. Previously very out-going, now she is somewhat reserved. Is a pupil at another school. Lives some distance from the Club and comes over by bicycle. Has never been exactly a popular member of the Club.

Captain of Football team
Bradley Thomas. Aged 17

Leaving school shortly, with no academic qualifications. Probably going to work for his father, who is a greengrocer. An all-round athlete, but not up to County standard. The football team has enjoyed a disastrous season - mainly because Brad had trouble most weeks in making up his strongest team. Has a regular succession of girl friends; regarded as a bit of a dog by his contemporaries.

RUNNING THE RESTAURANT

Possibly the most difficult of the lot, because many other skills are involved beyond acting. The group has to take over the entire restaurant - with the restaurant's real owner as cashier and overseeing that they don't make a muck of the whole thing.

The `cast' take over the entire `front of house' of the eatery, including the bar, and serve the customers to the best of their ability. `Back stage', of course, the normal kitchen staff labour on, plus a `chef' who will be implicated in the plot, after the unfortunate accident.

Obviously, the numbers involved will depend on the size of the restaurant and there might have to be some `real' waiters/waitresses and bar staff to supplement (and add a bit of professional stiffening) the group.

All this is pre-supposing a great deal of faith from the restaurant proprietor - so you will have to live up to your promises not to spill the soup down customers' necks or deposit vegetables in their laps! Whether the proprietor cares to become the interlocutor depends on him/her: perhaps this might be placing too much responsibility on someone who might well be distracted by witnessing non-professional behaviour by some of his `staff'.

The accident will happen to a solitary diner, who appeared to have been minding his own business until taking his `dive'.

There are no biographies offered, as the personnel will differ depending on the type of restaurant - general, ethnic, luxury - so you are on your own again. With a considerable number of problems.

☺☺●●☒☒

If you have enjoyed playing these improvisations and/or have tried variations based on them or completely new scenarios, the author would very much like to hear from you, so that a further collection might be offered to others.

A completely different sort of evening might be held, more 'theatrical' in feeling if the dinner party is distinctly different and it is obvious that they are going to be the entertainment for the evening. They might be dressed in period costume, for example. A situation which appeals is to have Henry VIII and all his six wives at dinner (historically impossible, but who cares?) and find out which of them - or a passing courtier - bumps him off, and why!

Please write to Ian Wilkes, c/o Ian Henry Publications, Ltd., 20 Park Drive, Romford, Essex RM1 4LH, England **or** c/o Players Press, Inc., P O Box 1132, Studio City, California 91614-0132, U S A; all suggestions will be gratefully received and, should publication ensue, acknowledged.

And here is another one, for luck...

THE LOTTERY WINNERS

This is just the barest bones of the characters, with scope for building the plot and the problems.

Leader of the syndicate
Joan Tree
Middle aged.
Has been going in for this weekly lottery for years and this is her first real win.
It is 'not going to change her life'.
Expects to keep on in the same job.

Also in the syndicate
Beryl Pertwee
Has only been a member of the syndicate since Helen quit three weeks ago.
Desperately wants the money so that she can help her sick mother.

The third member
Esther Bridges
Recently engaged.
Has plans to tell the boss what to do with the job and take a round-the-world cruise.

The leader's husband
Bill Tree
Unassuming.
Works for the same company as the others in the accounts department.
Would like to invest the winnings in a shop somewhere.

The lady who had just left the syndicate
Helen Adams
Was a member of the syndicate for years until recently, when she left saying that it was never going to pay off!

The syndicate's boss at work
Norma(n) Oliver
Going to retire shortly, having spent all working life with company.

The third member's boy friend
David Banks
Very earnest.
Works for a company that supplies 'our' company with materials.

A representative of the lottery
Nigel(a) Runciman
The problem is that we don't know (yet) if the syndicate have won an enormous sum - or if something was wrong with their entry and that this dinner is a sort of consolation prize.

PLAYERS PRESS CLASSIC PLAYS

THREE SISTERS ISBN 0-88734-705-3
Classic Anton Chekhov drama, edited and Introduction by William-Alan Landes. Cast of fourteen (9m, 5f). Three sisters in a distant garrison town search for the meaning of life after the death of their father.

THE TRAGEDY OF JANE SHORE ISBN 0-88734-295-7
A domestic tragedy by Nicholas Rowe, with Introduction by William-Alan Landes. The tale of an aging and flirtatious beauty, doomed by a liaison with the Crown.

UNCLE VANYA ISBN 0-88734-707-X
Drama by Anton Chekhov, edited and Introduction by William-Alan Landes. Cast of nine (5m, 4f). Forlorn passions and jealousies color the lives of a Russian family, culminating in violence and despair.

LADY WINDEMERE'S FAN ISBN 0-88734-278-7
Introduction by William-Alan Landes. Cast of sixteen (7m, 9f). Oscar Wilde's intense, thought-provoking play about a family's scandal as Lady Windemere's notorious mother returns home.

A DOLL'S HOUSE ISBN 0-88734-269-8
Drama by Henrik Ibsen. Cast of eleven (4m, 4f, 2b, 1g). A manipulated wife loves so deeply that she commits forgery; then faces her independent spirit and determine to leave her husband.

MEDEA ISBN 0-88734-253-1
Classic Greek tragedy by Euripedes, translated by Michael Woodhull, with Introduction by William-Alan Landes. Cast of nine (5m, 2f, 2b) plus chorus. Medea has sacrificed much for her love ... even betraying her father. Now her husband Jason is in love with Corinth. Medea seeks her revenge! A complex, compelling and magnificent love story.

LYSISTRATA ISBN 0-88734-345-7
Delightful classic Greek comedy by Aristophanes, translated by S.H. Landes. Cast of ten (4m, 5f, 1b/g) plus chorus and extras. Lysistrata organizes a campaign to end a war by persuading her fellow women to withhold their favors from their soldiering men.

(see current catalogue for prices)